D1713124

Cultural Celebrations

PASSOVER

DiscoverRoo
An Imprint of Pop!
popbooksonline.com

Susan E. Hamen

abdobooks.com

Published by Pop!, a division of ABDO, PO Box 398166, Minneapolis, Minnesota 55439. Copyright © 2021 by POP, LLC. International copyrights reserved in all countries. No part of this book may be reproduced in any form without written permission from the publisher. Pop!™ is a trademark and logo of POP, LLC.

Printed in the United States of America, North Mankato, Minnesota.

052020
092020

THIS BOOK CONTAINS
RECYCLED MATERIALS

Cover Photo: iStockphoto
Interior Photos: iStockphoto, 1, 9, 17, 19, 22 (top), 22 (bottom), 23 (top), 23 (bottom), 26, 27, 29, 30; Lou Toman/KRT/Newscom, 5; Shutterstock Images, 6–7, 11, 14, 15, 18, 20, 21, 28 31; Timewatch Images/Alamy, 10; Artokoloro/Alamy, 12–13; Tricia Spaulding/Athens Banner-Herald/AP Images, 25

Editor: Connor Stratton
Series Designer: Jake Slavik

Content Consultant: Samuel J. Kessler, PhD, Assistant Professor of Religion, Gustavus Adolphus College

Library of Congress Control Number: 2019954996
Publisher's Cataloging-in-Publication Data

Names: Hamen, Susan E., author.

Title: Passover / by Susan E. Hamen

Description: Minneapolis, Minnesota : POP!, 2021 | Series: Cultural celebrations | Includes online resources and index.

Identifiers: ISBN 9781532167713 (lib. bdg.) | ISBN 9781532168819 (ebook)

Subjects: LCSH: Passover--Juvenile literature. | Fasts and feasts--Judaism--Juvenile literature. | Passover--Customs and practices--Juvenile literature. | Holidays--Juvenile literature. | Social customs--Juvenile literature.

Classification: DDC 296.4/37--dc23

WELCOME TO
DiscoverRoo!

Pop open this book and you'll find QR codes loaded with information, so you can learn even more!

Scan this code* and others like it while you read, or visit the website below to make this book pop!

popbooksonline.com/passover

*Scanning QR codes requires a web-enabled smart device with a QR code reader app and a camera.

TABLE OF CONTENTS

CHAPTER 1
Preparing for Passover............ 4

CHAPTER 2
History of Passover 8

CHAPTER 3
The Days of Passover 16

CHAPTER 4
The Seder 24

Making Connections............. 30
Glossary 31
Index.......................... 32
Online Resources 32

CHAPTER 1
PREPARING FOR PASSOVER

A family gathers in the kitchen. Passover will begin when the sun sets. To prepare, the family makes **unleavened** bread. This bread is known as matzo. The family makes matzo ball soup as well. Someone

WATCH A VIDEO HERE!

Matzo ball soup is a dish first made by Jewish people in Europe.

finds the Haggadah. This is the Jewish

guide to the holiday's **rituals** and stories.

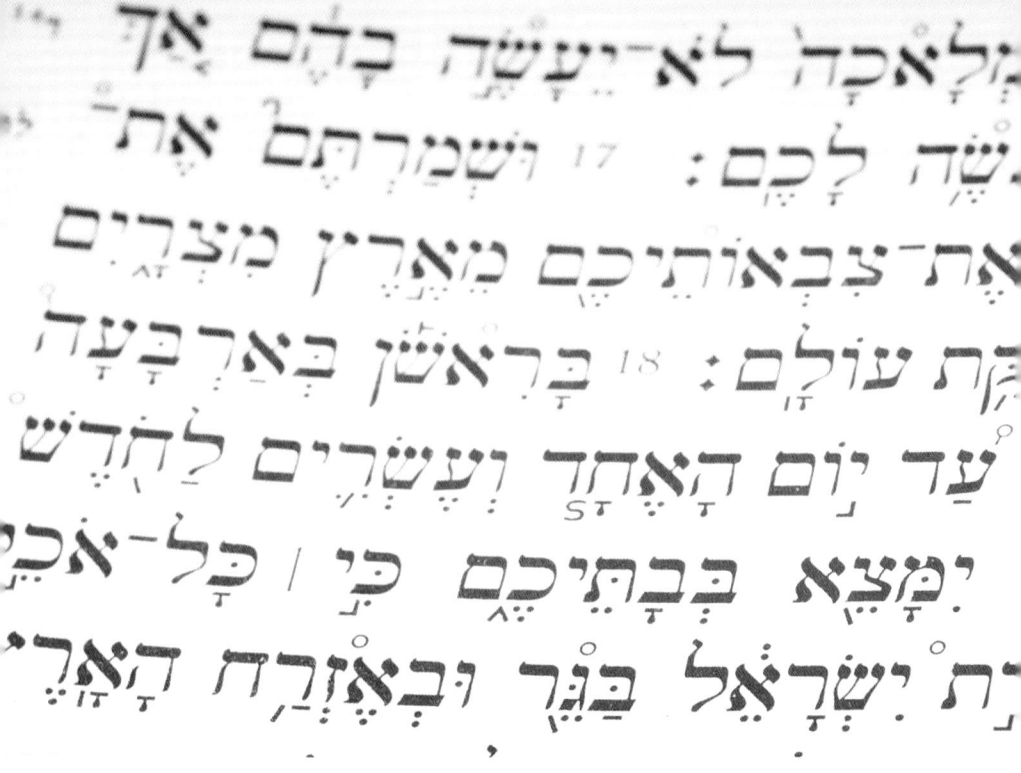

Passover is an important Jewish

holiday. Jews celebrate it every spring.

The holiday lasts for eight days. During

this time, Jews remember the story of

their **ancestors**. These people were freed

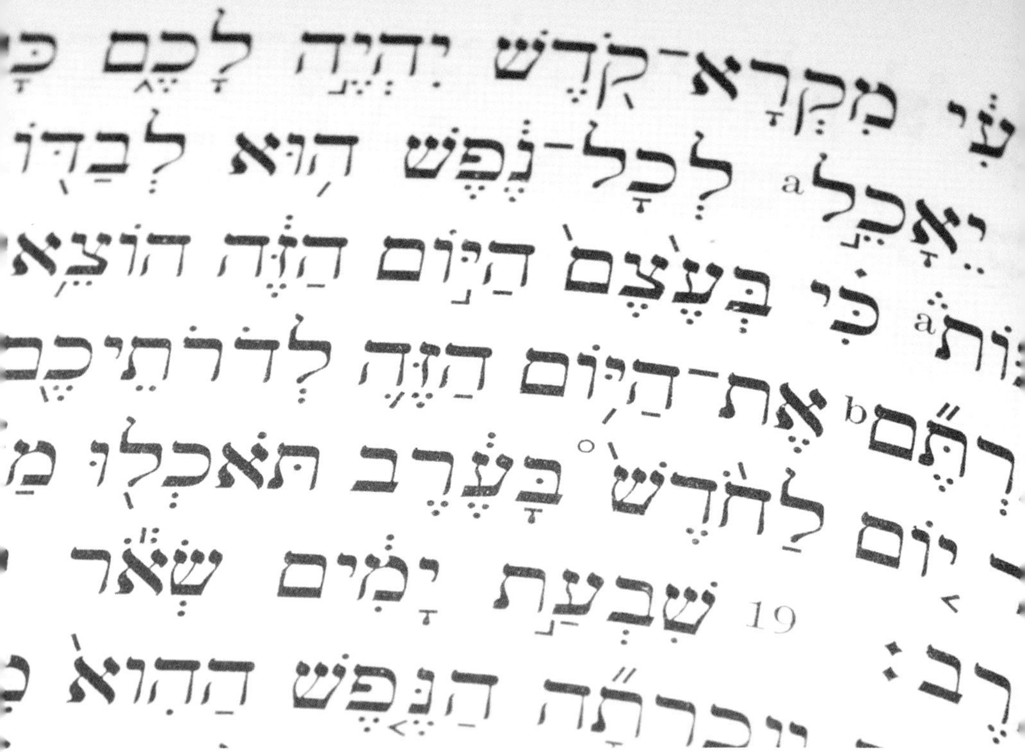

מִקְרָא־קֹדֶשׁ יִהְיֶה לָכֶם כִּ֫
לְכָל־נֶפֶשׁ הוּא לְבַדּ֫וֹ
בְּעֶצֶם הַיּוֹם הַזֶּה הוֹצֵ֫א
אֶת־הַיּוֹם הַזֶּה לְדֹרֹתֵיכֶ֫ם
בָּעֶרֶב תֹּאכְלוּ מַ֫
שִׁבְעַת יָמִים שְׂאֹר
19
וְנִכְרְתָה הַנֶּפֶשׁ הַהִוא

The Torah was first written in the ancient language of Hebrew.

from **slavery**. This story appears in the

Book of Exodus in the Torah. The Torah is

the Jewish holy book.

DID YOU KNOW?

Passover is called *Pesach* in Hebrew. This word means "to pass over."

CHAPTER 2
HISTORY OF PASSOVER

Thousands of years ago, people in Israel held festivals in spring. They traveled to local places of worship. Later, people went to the Holy Temple in Jerusalem. Each family **sacrificed** an animal there.

LEARN MORE HERE!

These people also ate matzo for seven days to celebrate their history and the coming harvest. This holiday became known as Passover.

Matzo is a thin, flat bread made from flour and water.

According to the Book of Exodus, Moses led the Jews out of Egypt by parting the Red Sea.

Jews began to tell the story of

Exodus. People told how God freed their

ancestors from slavery. This story was important for the ancient Jews. Over time, celebrating the story became its own holiday.

THE SECOND BOOK OF MOSES, CALLED

EXODUS

CHAPTER 1

NOW these are the names of the children of Is'ra-el, which came into Egypt; every man and his household came with Ja'cob.

2 Reu'ben, Sim'e-on, Le'vi, and Ju'dah,

3 Is'sa-char, Zeb'u-lun, and Ben'ja-min,

4 Dan, and Naph'ta-li, Gad, and Ash'er.

5 And all the souls that ... the loins of Ja ...

office of a midwife to the He women, and see them upon the if it be a son, then ye shall but if it be a daughter, then she live.

17 But the midwives, th and did not as

commanded th children al

18 A

Jews traveled to Jerusalem for

Passover for nearly 1,000 years. They

brought sacrifices. They ate matzo.

In 70 CE, the Romans destroyed the

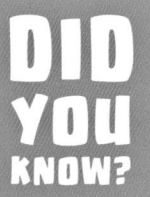

In addition to destroying the Holy Temple, the Romans destroyed the city of Jerusalem.

Holy Temple. They scattered the

Jewish people. As a result, Passover

changed too.

DID YOU KNOW?

Some parts of Judaism date back more than 3,000 years.

Jews started celebrating the

holiday in their homes. People stopped

sacrificing animals. Instead, Jewish

A family gathers for the Passover Seder.

People of all ages participate in the Seder.

leaders known as rabbis created the

Seder. During this meal, people told the

story of the Exodus. They used **rituals**,

stories, and music.

CHAPTER 3
THE DAYS OF PASSOVER

The Torah tells Jews to honor the first and

last days of Passover as holy days. These

days are days of complete rest. Jews

often do not go to work. Not working is

LEARN MORE
HERE!

important. Jews can spend all their time

observing the day's **rituals** and joys.

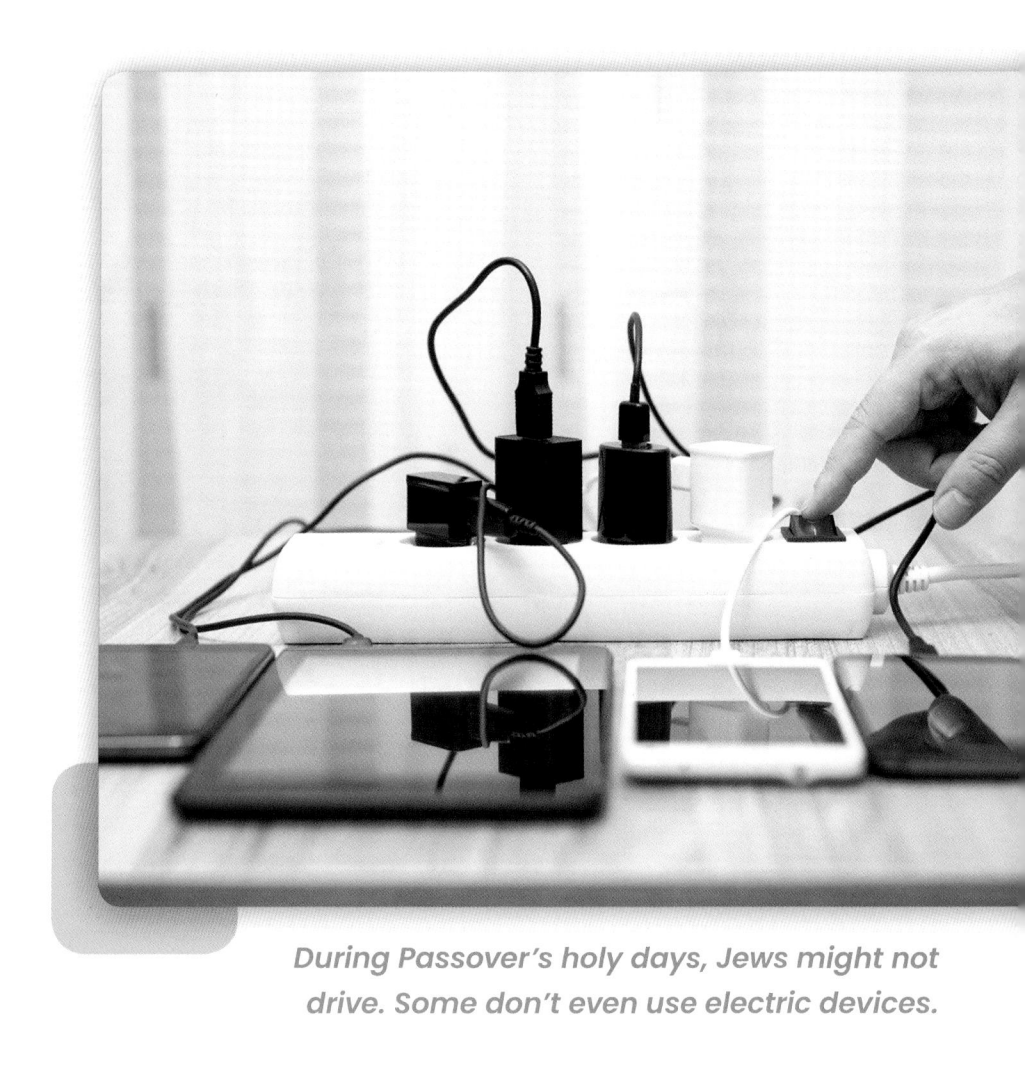

*During Passover's holy days, Jews might not
drive. Some don't even use electric devices.*

The word synagogue comes from a Greek word that means "to bring together."

Passover's middle days are called Chol Hamoed. Work is allowed. But celebrations still happen. Some families go to museums or parks. Others go to their **synagogue**. They pray there. People might also hear readings from the Torah.

A rabbi typically leads the service at the synagogue.

Common chametz products include bread, crackers, and pasta.

The Torah explains how the Jews left Egypt. The book says the Jews ate **unleavened** bread. So, people do not eat leavened grains during the holiday.

These foods are called chametz. Before the holiday, Jews often throw out all of these kinds of foods.

Before Passover, some Jews burn chametz in a cleansing ritual.

DID YOU KNOW?

During Passover, many people do not even feed their pets chametz products.

CELEBRATING PASSOVER

BEFORE PASSOVER

Jews get rid of all chametz products in their homes.

DAYS 1 AND 2

People rest during the first two days. They also have a feast known as the Seder.

DAYS 3 THROUGH 6

The middle days are Chol Hamoed. People can do some work. Many families spend time together. They also attend their synagogues.

DAYS 7 AND 8

Jews rest during the last two days. They pray and prepare food for the holiday's final meals. On Day 7, Jews also retell the story of Moses parting the Red Sea.

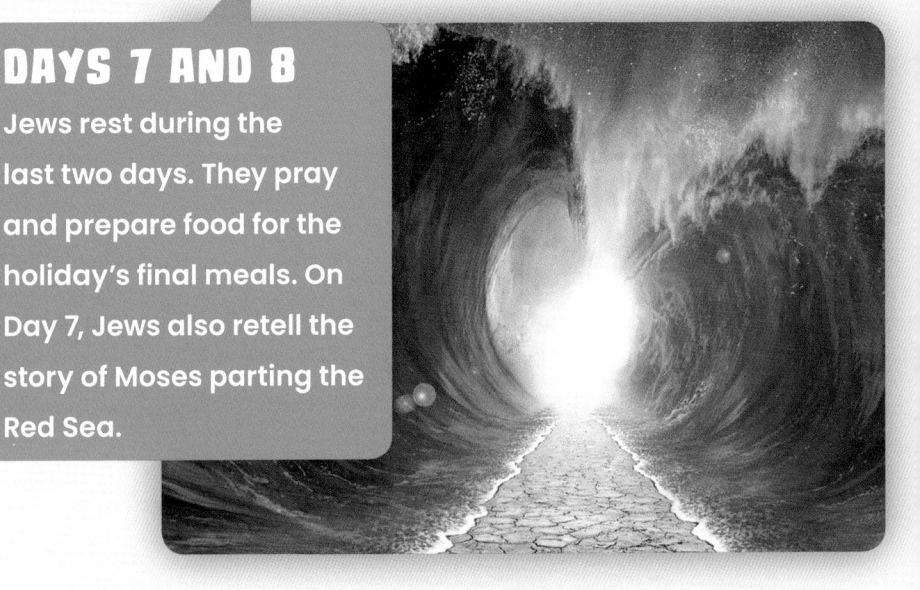

CHAPTER 4

THE SEDER

Jewish families have a feast the first night of Passover. This dinner is known as the Seder. Outside of Israel, families may have the Seder the second night as well. The meal begins after nightfall.

COMPLETE AN ACTIVITY HERE!

Seders can include gatherings of families and friends.

People set out the Seder plate. The plate holds five or six foods. One is a fruit and nut paste called charoset. These foods stand for parts of the Passover story. For example, bitter herbs stand for the bitterness of **slavery**. A lamb bone stands for animals that Jews used to **sacrifice**.

Seder plate

ITEMS ON THE SEDER PLATE

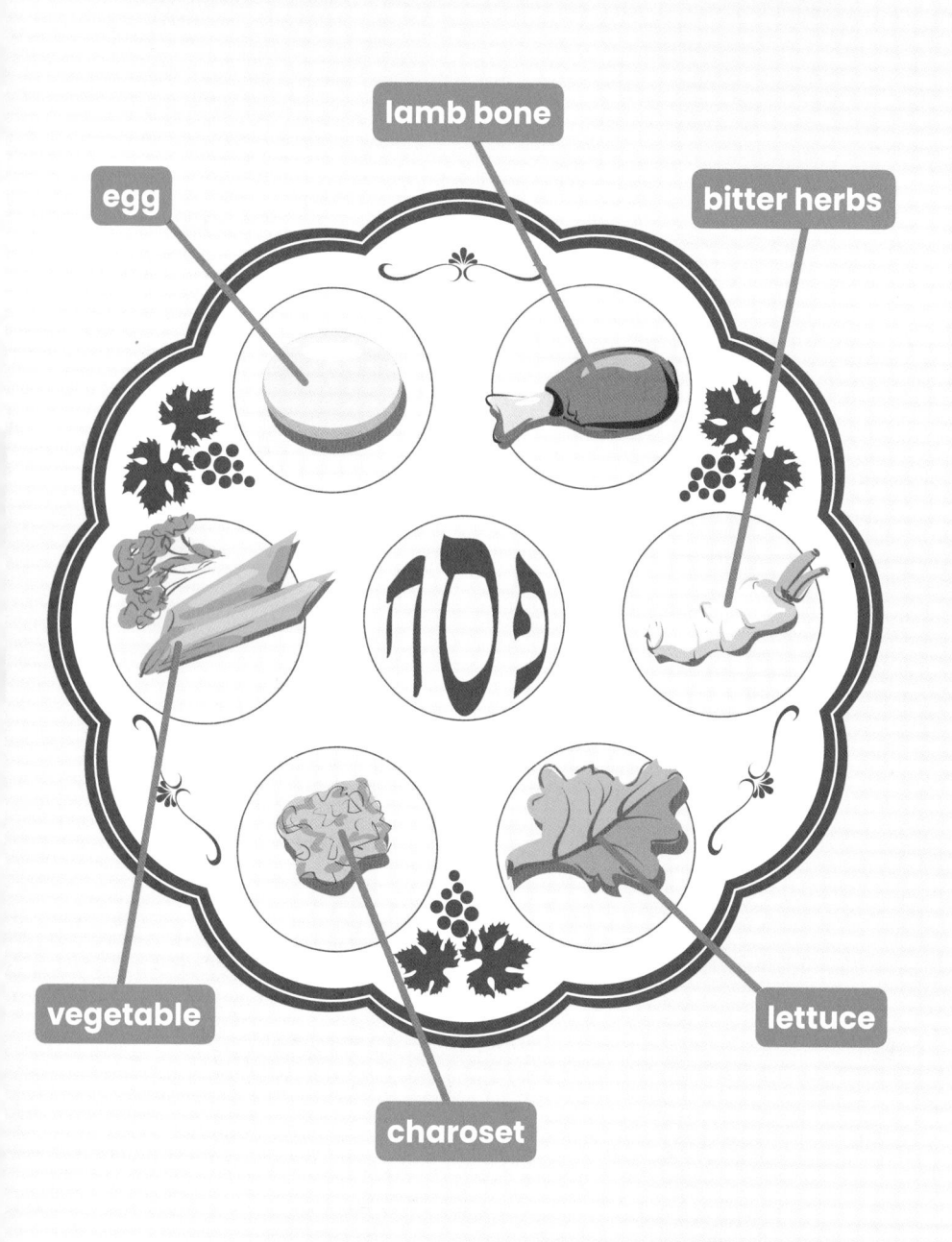

People break matzo in the fourth step of the Seder.

A Seder has 15 steps. Some steps include eating matzo and washing hands. People eat the Seder plate's items. The youngest child also asks four questions. These questions help people remember the holiday's main ideas. Then, someone tells the story of Exodus.

The four questions are asked in the fifth step of the Seder.

DID YOU KNOW?

A book known as the Haggadah explains the steps in the Seder.

MAKING CONNECTIONS

TEXT-TO-SELF

Passover Seders have many steps and
traditions. Are there any events in your life that
follow certain traditions?

TEXT-TO-TEXT

Have you read books about other holidays?
What do they have in common with Passover?
How are they different?

TEXT-TO-WORLD

The story of Exodus is important to Passover.
What stories can you think of that are important
to other holidays?

GLOSSARY

ancestor – a family member who lived long ago.

plague – an extremely harmful disease or event.

ritual – a set of actions with special meaning.

sacrifice – to offer something important to a god to receive protection or power.

slavery – a system where certain people are owned by other people.

synagogue – a Jewish place of worship.

unleavened – having to do with food made from grains that have not been allowed to rise.

INDEX

chametz, 21, 22

Chol Hamoed, 19, 23

Egypt, 11, 20

Exodus, 7, 10, 11, 15, 28

Haggadah, 5, 29

Hebrew, 7

Jerusalem, 8, 12

matzo, 4, 9, 12, 28

Seder, 15, 22, 24, 26, 27, 28–29

synagogues, 19, 23

Torah, 7, 11, 16, 19–20

ONLINE RESOURCES

popbooksonline.com

Scan this code* and others like it while you read, or visit the website below to make this book pop!

popbooksonline.com/passover

*Scanning QR codes requires a web-enabled smart device with a QR code reader app and a camera.